Managing Editor
Karen J. Goldfluss, M.S. Ed.

Editor-in-Chief
Sharon Coan, M.S. Ed.

Illustrators
Howard Chaney
Bruce Hedges

Cover Artist
Lesley Palmer

Art Coordinator
Kevin Barnes

Art Director
CJae Froshay

Imaging
Alfred Lau
James Edward Grace

Product Manager
Phil Garcia

Publisher
Mary D. Smith, M.S. Ed.

Rocks Minerals

SUPER SCIENCE ACTIVITIES

Color   Luster   Streak   Texture   Hardness

Written by Ruth M. Young, M.S. Ed.

Teacher Created Resources

Teacher Created Resources, Inc.
6421 Industry Way
Westminster, CA 92683
www.teachercreated.com

ISBN: 978-0-7439-3666-8

©2002 Teacher Created Resources, Inc.
Reprinted, 2009

Made in the U.S.A.

Table of Contents

Introduction

Rocks cover the entire surface of Earth, even beneath every body of water and the polar ice caps. This rock covering is referred to as the *crust* of Earth. Dirt or soil, which consists of crushed rock and pieces of once living (*organic*) material, covers some areas of the crust.

Earth's crust consists of three types of rock—*igneous*, *sedimentary*, and *metamorphic*. These rocks do not remain as one type but are continuously being recycled from one type to another.

Igneous

Melted rock beneath the crust, called *magma*, is under tremendous pressure and sometimes rises through cracks in the crust. Magma may cool underground within the crust or break through the crust and pour onto the surface in the form of liquid rock called *lava*. When the magma or lava solidifies, it is called *igneous* rock. The crust is cracked into large sections called *plates*. The edges of some crustal plates are forced beneath other plates, melting and recycling the leading edge of rock as it comes into contact with the hot magma.

Sedimentary

These rocks consist of crushed rocks which were once igneous, metamorphic, or sedimentary. This crushed rock material is deposited in layers by wind, water, or ice. As the layers build up, the pressure packs the material together until it compresses into solid rock layers. These sediments may consist of rock fragments ranging in size from large boulders to fine grains of sand and silt. Sedimentary rocks may also be deposits of minerals in the form of crystals or organic material such as shells.

Metamorphic

This type of rock changes or undergoes a *metamorphosis* due to tremendous pressure when it is buried deep in the earth's crust. It can also be changed due to the heat of magma when it comes close to the rock layer but not close enough to melt the rock. Metamorphic rock began as igneous, sedimentary, or metamorphic rock. The original rock changes in appearance and often in mineral composition. For example, the igneous rock *granite* changes to the metamorphic rock *gneiss*, and the sedimentary rock *limestone* changes to the metamorphic rock *marble*.

✧

The activities in this book will enable students to develop an understanding of the rock cycle and the differences between rocks and minerals. They will also learn how to identify minerals.

An Ant's Eye View of Soil

Overview: *Students will examine a variety of soil samples.*

Materials (for each student)

- snack-size resealable bags
- magnifying lenses
- transparency and copies of What Is Soil? (pages 6 and 7)
- parent letter (page 5)
- plastic spoons

Lesson Preparation

- Make copies of the parent letter and attach a plastic bag to each note. Write students' names on the bags.
- A day or two before doing this activity, give each student a plastic bag and parent letter. Explain what they are to put in the bag and when they need to return the sample to school. Send home the letter and bag.

Activity: Day One

1. Ask the students what they call the "stuff" which is found on the ground (*dirt*). Explain that this can also be called *soil* and that they are going to go on a walk around the school area to collect different samples of soil.

2. Take the students into the schoolyard to find different types of soil samples. Look for a variety of areas to dig up samples, such as a grass area, a field of native plants, or dry soil without any vegetation. Collect samples in bags and write where each was found. (**Caution:** Students need to wear vinyl gloves or wash their hands with soap each time they are finished working with soil samples.)

3. Return to the classroom and explain that these specimens will be used during the next science class. Explain that the students will need to bring in their soil samples from home so that the different specimens can be compared with those collected around the school area.

Activity: Day Two

1. Divide students into groups of four. Give each student a magnifier, plastic spoon, and a copy of page 6 and 7 the two worksheets. Have the students put a plastic spoon into each bag with the soil specimen.

2. Discuss the difference between living or once-living things and things which were never alive. Give them examples of these two categories and write some of these on the board.

3. Use a transparency and copies of pages 6 and 7 to demonstrate how to use the spoon to place a small sample of one soil specimen in the circle. Show how to write the location where the sample was collected.

4. Monitor students as they complete the data for their first specimen.

5. Have students examine three other specimens and write their observations. Give them clear tape to place over their specimens to preserve their samples.

Closure

- Discuss what students found in their soil samples. Compare these with the materials found in the school soil samples. Save the worksheets for the students' rocks and minerals journals.

Parent Letter for Soil Samples

Date_____

Dear Parents,

We have begun a study of rocks and minerals, and our first activity will be to look at different samples of soil. The students will examine these samples with magnifiers to see if they can find out what makes soil.

Please help your child partially fill the attached small bag with a soil sample. This may be taken from the yard or a houseplant. Write where the sample was collected and your child's name on the label below and place it inside the bag.

It is important that the child bring the bag back to school by_____ so the soil can be examined during our science class time.

Be sure to ask your child what he or she learned from this activity after we have looked at the specimens. You are welcome to join us. We will be examining our specimens on_____at_____.

Thanks for helping your child add to our science study of dirt.

Cordially,

_____

Soil Sample

Collected by _____
                                    student name

Collected from _____

_____

_____

An Ant's Eye View of Soil *(cont.)*

What Is Soil?

Name:_____ Date:_____

Fill in the information needed below:

Location: _____

Color:_____

Feel:_____

Living or once-living things which
I found in this soil:

_____

_____

Things which were never alive which
I found in this soil:

_____

_____

Sample #1

Location: _____

Color:_____

Feel:_____

Living or once-living things which
I found in this soil:

_____

_____

Things which were never alive which
I found in this soil:

_____

_____

Sample #2

What Is Soil? (cont.)

Name: _____ Date: _____

Fill in the information needed below:

Location: _____

Color: _____

Feel: _____

Living or once-living things which
I found in this soil:

_____

_____

Things which were never alive which
I found in this soil:

_____

_____

Sample #3

Location: _____

Color: _____

Feel: _____

Living or once-living things which
I found in this soil:

_____

_____

Things which were never alive which
I found in this soil:

_____

_____

Sample #4

Let's Eat Dirt

Overview: *Students will use edible materials to simulate dirt.*

Materials

- chocolate cookies, two per student
- one cup (240 mL) powdered sugar
- four cups (1L) milk
- two cups (480 mL) raisins
- eight-ounce (240 mL) package of softened cream cheese
- ½ cup (120 mL) margarine or softened butter
- jellied sugar worms, one per student
- chocolate sprinkles
- two 4-ounce (120 mL) packages of instant chocolate pudding
- eight-ounce (240 mL) container of whipped topping
- clear plastic drinking straw, one per student
- clear plastic 6-ounce (180 mL) cup
- snack-size resealable plastic bag for each student
- small paper bowls, two per group
- plastic spoons, one per student
- heavy book

Activity

1. Discuss what the students found in their soil samples in the previous lesson. Tell them that in this lesson, they are going to make dirt which they can eat.

2. Distribute to each student one plastic bag and two chocolate cookies. Tell them to place the cookies inside the plastic bag, press out the air, and then zip it closed.

3. Have each student place a book over the plastic bag and press hard until the cookies are crushed into small pieces. Tell them the cookies are rocks which they are breaking into tiny pieces to make dirt.

4. Divide the students into groups to assist in preparing the following:

   - Cream together the softened cream cheese, butter, and powdered sugar.
   - Fold the whipped topping into the creamed mixture.
   - Beat the milk into the instant pudding.

Let's Eat Dirt (cont.)

Activity (cont.)

5. Distribute separate bowls of the creamed and pudding mixtures to each group.

6. Give each group raisins, jellied worms, and chocolate sprinkles. Explain that the raisins are small rocks, the jellied worms are earthworms, and the chocolate sprinkles are small insects like ants.

7. Give every student a plastic cup and have each place a thin layer of crushed cookies at the bottom of the cup. Have them spoon alternating layers of the creamed and pudding mixtures. They should also add thin layers of crushed cookies, raisins, and sprinkles between the layers. The worm can be added to any layer and covered over. The last layer should be of cookie crumbs.

8. Chill the cups of "dirt" until they are set.

Closure

• Distribute the chilled dirt to the students and give each of them a drinking straw. Have them push the straw into the mixture and pull out a sample. Have them look at the different layers they see inside the straw. Explain that this is just what they see when they drive through a road cut—the layers of rock and dirt that were laid down over millions of years.

• Let the students enjoy eating their "dirt" samples.

Mini-Rocks

Overview: *Students will examine a variety of sand samples to learn where they come from.*

Materials

- transparency and two copies per student of page 12
- magnifying lens for each student
- white glue which dries clear
- sand samples
- copies of parent letter (page 11)
- snack-size resealable plastic bags (one per student)
- toothpicks (one per student)
- waxed paper (small, 4"/10 cm square per student)

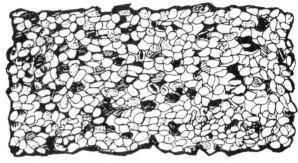

Lesson Preparation

- Make copies of the parent letter and staple a bag to each of them. Distribute these at least a week prior to doing this lesson.

- Contact construction supply stores to see if they can provide some unusual sand samples. Collect some sand from the school sandbox. Label all the bags of sand specimens with the location from which they came, including those brought to school by students.

- Place a few drops of white glue in the center of the waxed paper.

Activity

1. Review what students found soil is made of and ask them what they think sand is.

2. Distribute a copy of the worksheet to each student. Divide the students into small groups and give each of them sand samples.

3. Show the students how to use the toothpick to transfer a few drops of glue and then spread it over the center of the rectangle on the work sheet. Show them how to sprinkle the sand sample over the glue and then let it dry.

4. After the glue dries, demonstrate how the students should use their magnifier to enlarge the sand grains to see their shapes. Tell them to write the colors they see in the sand.

6. Let the students examine at least four different sand samples. (**Note:** Be sure the students wash their hands with soap after handling the sand samples.)

Closure

- Have students share what they saw when they examined the sand.

- Ask them how they think sand is made. (*Rocks are broken into smaller pieces by water, wind, and pressure.*)

Parent Letter for Sand Samples

Date_____

Dear Parents,

We appreciated the soil samples you sent to school for our science class. The students learned that soil is made up of crushed rocks, as well as things which at one time were alive, such as insects or leaves. Now, we are ready to take a closer look at sand to see if we can find what it is made of.

If you have any sand samples to offer, please put a small amount in the attached bag. On the label below, write where the sample was collected and your child's name and place it inside the bag.

It is important that the child bring the bag back to school by_____
so the sand can be examined during our science class time.

Be sure to ask your child what he or she learned from this activity after we have looked at the samples. You are welcome to join us. We will be examining the sand
on_____at_____.

Thanks for helping your child add to our science study of sand.

Cordially,

_____

Sand Sample

Collected by _____
student name

Collected from _____

_____

_____

Mini-Rocks (cont.)

Teeny Tiny Rocks

Name: _____ Date: _____

Fill in the information below:

I see the colors _____.

This sand feels _____.

This sand came from _____.

Put the tape across the box and put a pinch of sand on it.

When I looked at the sand through a magnifier, it looked like this.

Fill in the information below:

I see the colors _____.

This sand feels _____.

This sand came from _____.

Put the tape across the box and put a pinch of sand on it.

When I looked at the sand through a magnifier, it looked like this.

Earth's Layers

Crust of the Earth

Overview: *Students will discover that Earth is made of layers, somewhat similar to a hard-boiled egg.*

Materials

- hard-boiled egg
- permanent black marker

Activity

1. Have each student draw what they think Earth would look like if it were cut in half.

2. Save these drawings to be used again after this lesson is finished.

Demonstration

1. Cut a hard-boiled egg in half lengthwise and use the black marker to make a dot in the center of the egg.

2. Explain that Earth is somewhat like this egg, with the crust being the egg's shell, the white layer representing the mantle, the yolk representing the core, and the black dot being the inner core.

3. Crack the shell to show how Earth's crust is cracked. Tell the students that this is due to pressure of the mantle pushing upward against the crust, cracking it in some areas.

4. Tell students that the egg shell is actually too thick to represent Earth's crust. Remove the shell and color the outside of the egg with a felt pen. This layer of coloring would represent the actual thickness of the crust in comparison to the rest of Earth.

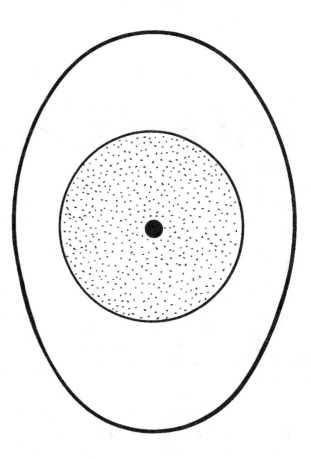

Closure

- Do the Earth Pizza activity.

Earth's Layers *(cont.)*

Earth Pizza

Overview: *Students will make a model cross section of Earth, formed by spirals of colored ropes of modeling compound.*

Materials

- small containers of red, yellow, blue, and brown tempera paint
- five toothpicks or T-pins for flags
- Earth Pizza Flags (page 16)
- ruler
- compass (for drawing circles)
- round pizza cardboard at least 14 inches (36 cm) in diameter
- transparency of page 18
- one pound of Crayola Model Magic® Modeling Compound (available at craft store)

Activity

1. Use the chart below to see how many students to assign to each section.

Scale Model of the Earth

Section	Number of Ropes	Size	Color
Inner Core	1 to form a disk	2.5 '' (6.4 cm) diameter	red
Outer Core	9–10	2.1'' (5.3 cm) band	red-yellow = orange
Core/Mantle Boundary	1.5–2	thin band	red-blue = purple
Lower Mantle	35	2.1'' (5.3 cm) band	yellow
Upper Mantle	7	.5'' (1.3 cm) band	pink (slightly red)
Crust	none	thickness of paint	blue (oceans)
			some brown (land)

2. Draw circles on the cardboard, beginning in the center for the inner core. Mark distances for the other sections from the outside edge of the last band. Keep the point of the compass in the center to draw the next circle. Continue until the four circles are drawn.

3. Make each rope from a ball (about one-inch diameter) of modeling compound. Flatten the ball and place drops of one or two colors to create the desired tint. Fold and knead the compound to distribute color. Take a pea-size piece of the ball and roll into a very thin rope. Link each rope to the previous one, coiling out from the center.

4. The inner core is made first and laid in the center of the cardboard. Add orange ropes to the outer edge to fill the circle for the outer core. Smooth the coils to join them together.

5. Add colored ropes until all sections are filled.

6. The crust layer is painted on the outer edge, using blue for oceans and some brown for land above sea level.

Earth's Layers *(cont.)*

Earth Pizza (cont.)

Closure

- Discuss the thickness of each section with the class to help them realize how thin the crust is compared to the rest of the earth.

- Place a marker for each section, using a flag made from a small triangle cut from a file card. This flag should have the name of the section, its thickness, temperature, and state of matter (e.g., solid) of the material. Hold the flags in place with toothpicks or T-pins.

- Use tempera paint to illustrate subduction of crustal plates and fountains of hot spots as shown in the illustration below.

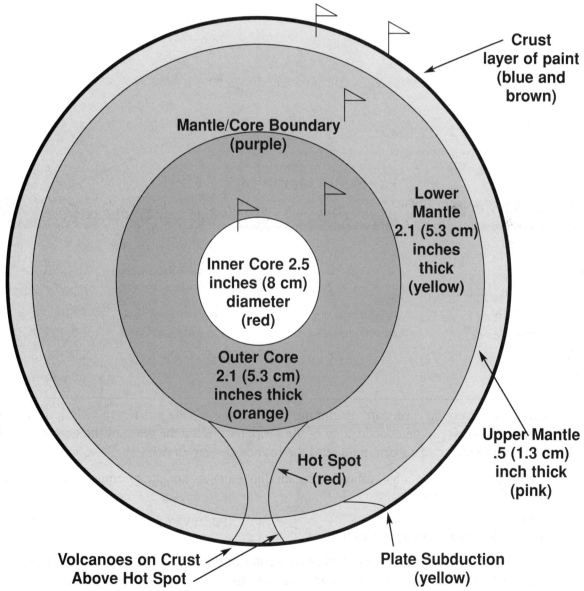

Crust layer of paint (blue and brown)

Mantle/Core Boundary (purple)

Lower Mantle 2.1 (5.3 cm) inches thick (yellow)

Inner Core 2.5 inches (8 cm) diameter (red)

Outer Core 2.1 (5.3 cm) inches thick (orange)

Upper Mantle .5 (1.3 cm) inch thick (pink)

Hot Spot (red)

Volcanoes on Crust Above Hot Spot

Plate Subduction (yellow)

Extender

The model will dry within 24 hours but remains soft and flexible. This "Earth Pizza" can be divided into sections with a knife or pizza cutter for each student to keep.

Earth Pizza Flags

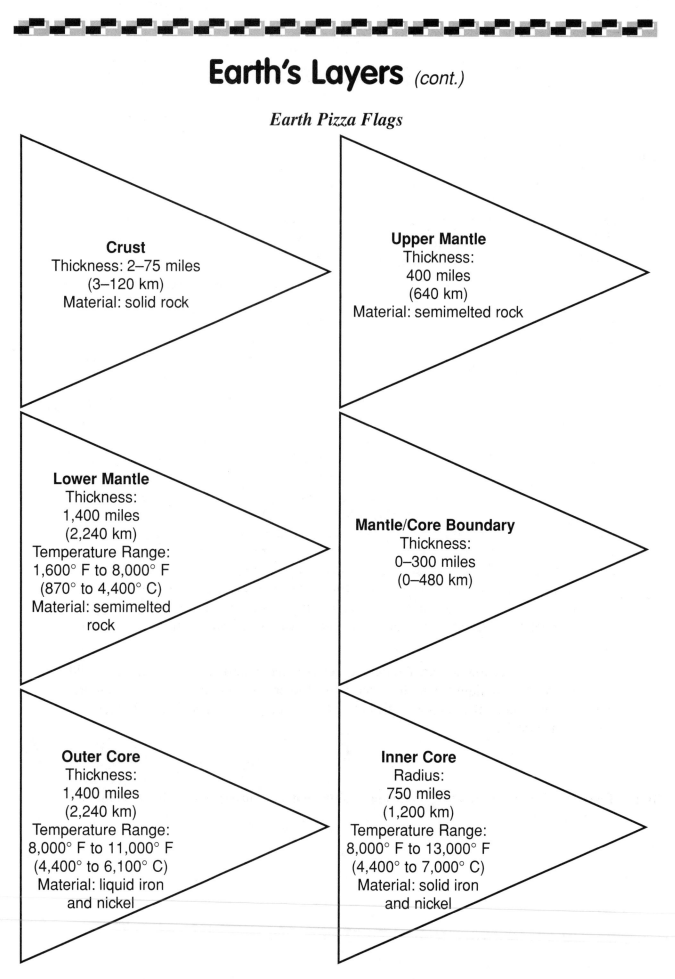

Crust
Thickness: 2–75 miles
(3–120 km)
Material: solid rock

Upper Mantle
Thickness:
400 miles
(640 km)
Material: semimelted rock

Lower Mantle
Thickness:
1,400 miles
(2,240 km)
Temperature Range:
1,600° F to 8,000° F
(870° to 4,400° C)
Material: semimelted
rock

Mantle/Core Boundary
Thickness:
0–300 miles
(0–480 km)

Outer Core
Thickness:
1,400 miles
(2,240 km)
Temperature Range:
8,000° F to 11,000° F
(4,400° to 6,100° C)
Material: liquid iron
and nickel

Inner Core
Radius:
750 miles
(1,200 km)
Temperature Range:
8,000° F to 13,000° F
(4,400° to 7,000° C)
Material: solid iron
and nickel

Earth's Layers *(cont.)*

The Inside of the Earth

Teacher Information

Earth is about 7,928 miles (12,685 km) in diameter. Most scientists believe Earth is divided into five layers: crust, upper mantle, lower mantle, outer core, and inner core. The inside view of Earth shown on page 18 gives information about these layers. The thinnest part of the crust is beneath the ocean; the thickest is beneath the continents.

Scientists know what the interior of Earth must be like from studying earthquake data. They measure how fast the earthquake waves travel through Earth and in what directions. The temperature and density of the material inside Earth can be calculated from this information. The mantle/core boundary is a division between the mantle and core. It varies in thickness as it is pulled and pushed by the lower mantle, moving in a swirling pattern caused by convection currents.

These convection currents are created when magma in the mantle gets near the core and is heated. It becomes less dense and, therefore, rises. Eventually, it meets the undersurface of the crust where it loses its heat and begins to descend again toward the core. This is just like a conveyor belt. The crust sits on top of the mantle and is pushed around by this action. Where weak spots occur, the magma can push through the crust, creating volcanoes. On the floor of the ocean there are cracks where magma pours out like toothpaste squeezed from a tube. The magma becomes lava which cools on contact with the ocean water and adds to the rock layers. The force of the convection currents in the magma also pushes the plates of the crust around, creating earthquakes as the plates push against each other and force up mountains at the contact point. The plates may also push under other plates; this is called *subduction*. The solid rock on the leading edge of the plate being subducted melts on contact with the magma in the mantle and is recycled.

It may seem strange that despite the inner core being the hottest layer of Earth, it is solid iron and nickel—not liquid as in the outer core. The pressure of the rest of Earth on the inner core is so great that the molecules of iron and nickel are packed so tightly they form solid crystals.

To the Teacher: Use the information on this page along with a transparency of the diagram on page 18 to teach students about the inside of Earth.

Earth's Layers *(cont.)*

The Inside of the Earth Diagram

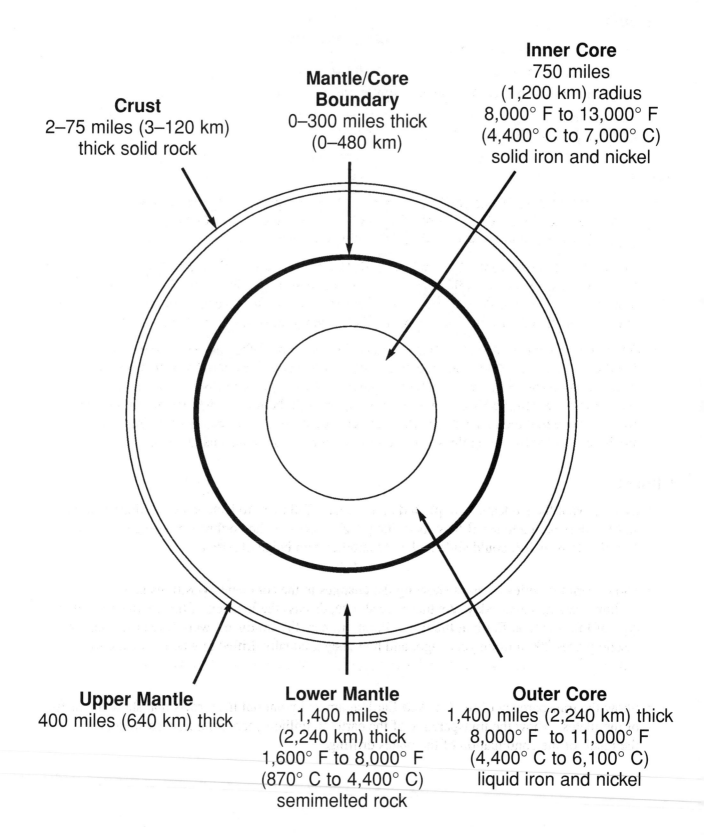

Crust
2–75 miles (3–120 km)
thick solid rock

Mantle/Core Boundary
0–300 miles thick
(0–480 km)

Inner Core
750 miles
(1,200 km) radius
8,000° F to 13,000° F
(4,400° C to 7,000° C)
solid iron and nickel

Upper Mantle
400 miles (640 km) thick

Lower Mantle
1,400 miles
(2,240 km) thick
1,600° F to 8,000° F
(870° C to 4,400° C)
semimelted rock

Outer Core
1,400 miles (2,240 km) thick
8,000° F to 11,000° F
(4,400° C to 6,100° C)
liquid iron and nickel

Cracked Earth

Overview: *Students will learn about the movement of Earth's tectonic plates.*

Materials

- transparency and student copies of page 20
- transparency of page 18
- red, green, and brown markers or crayons
- copy of page 21
- transparencies of 22–24

Activity

1. Remind the students of the cracked egg activity they did (page 13) which showed how thin the earth's crust is compared to the rest of it. Show them the transparency of the earth's layers | (page 18) and point out how the thin crust rests on the upper mantle.

2. Project the transparency of the Cracked Earth Map and point out the continents. Explain that the puzzle-like shapes are are called plates and, like the egg shell, they are outlined by cracks which go all the way down to the upper mantle. Tell the students that the continents are the part of the plates that stick up above the ocean floor. The ocean floor is also part of the plates.

3. Divide the students into small groups and distribute a copy of the map to each of them. Tell them that the first person to think that the earth's crust was cracked and moved around was laughed at since no one could see how something as gigantic as the continents could possibly move. Distribute the Scientific Evidence to each group and tell them that scientists have now gathered proof to show that the plates upon which the continents sit are indeed moving. Have them follow the directions for recording the scientific information on to the map using the crayons.

Closure

- Discuss what the students have plotted on the map. Tell them to look at the continents of Africa and South America to see if they look like puzzle pieces. (The northwestern bulge of South America look as if it could slide under the southeastern bulge of Africa.

- Show them the series of maps showing the changes in the continents' positions between 200 million years ago and today. As these are shown, discuss the location of the continents and the type of life found on Earth at the time. Point out how the continents were fitted together like puzzle pieces 200 million years ago, and how they gradually drifted to where they are today. Remind them of the evidence they have just plotted which proves this movement.

- Show the transparency of the Cracked Earth again and point out the arrows that show the drifting of the plates. Show the transparency of the earth 50 million years from now so students can see the result of the continuation of the plates drifting.

Map of Major Plates

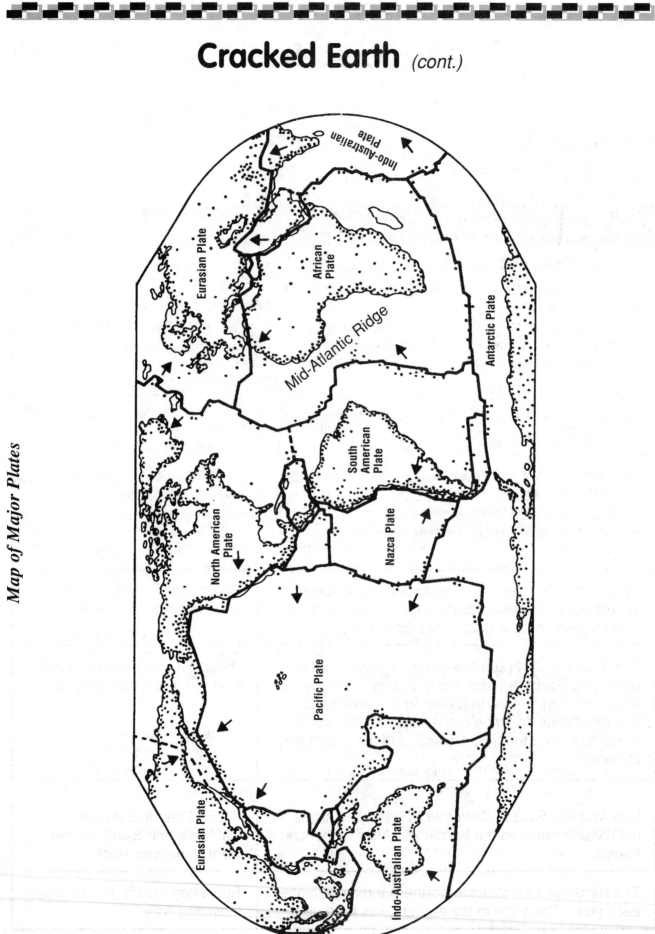

Cracked Earth *(cont.)*

Scientific Proof That Earth's Continents Drift

To the Students: You are scientists who are examining the evidence which has been collected to prove that the earth's crust is divided into plates which, have gradually moved the continents around. Carefully record this information on the Cracked Earth Map.

Scientific Evidence	Code
The same fossils of large land animals are found on the eastern edge of South America and the western edge of Africa.	Green line along the east coast of South America and west coast of Africa.
The same type and age of rock formations are found on the eastern edge of South America and the western edge of Africa.	Brown line along the east coast of South America and west coast of Africa.
Fossil remains of animals like those found in Australia have been discovered in Antarctica.	Green X's on both of these continents.
A long, high ridge runs north-south along the middle of the floor of the Atlantic Ocean. Rock samples taken along the top of this ridge show the rocks are younger than those taken further away from the ridge.	Red line outlining the mid-Atlantic ridge. Brown on the side of the ridges.
Deep-sea diving vessels investigating areas along the ridges discovered molten magma pushing up. This magma cools and becomes new rock.	Red along the west and south edge of the Nazca Plate.
The mountains that run along the western coast of North and South America are gradually rising higher. There are frequent earthquakes in this area also. The mountains on these coasts also contain active volcanoes, like Mount St. Helens, and many dormant volcanoes.	Red along the western coasts of North and South America.
Earthquakes happen frequently along and near the San Andreas Fault in California. This fault outlines the division between the Pacific and North American Plates.	Red along the edge of the Pacific Plate that divides California and Baja from the North American Plate.
The Himalaya Mountains in northern India rise higher each year. There are many earthquakes here also.	Red along the division between India and Asia.

Cracked Earth (cont.)

Earth's Continents: Then, Now, and Beyond

200 Million Years Ago

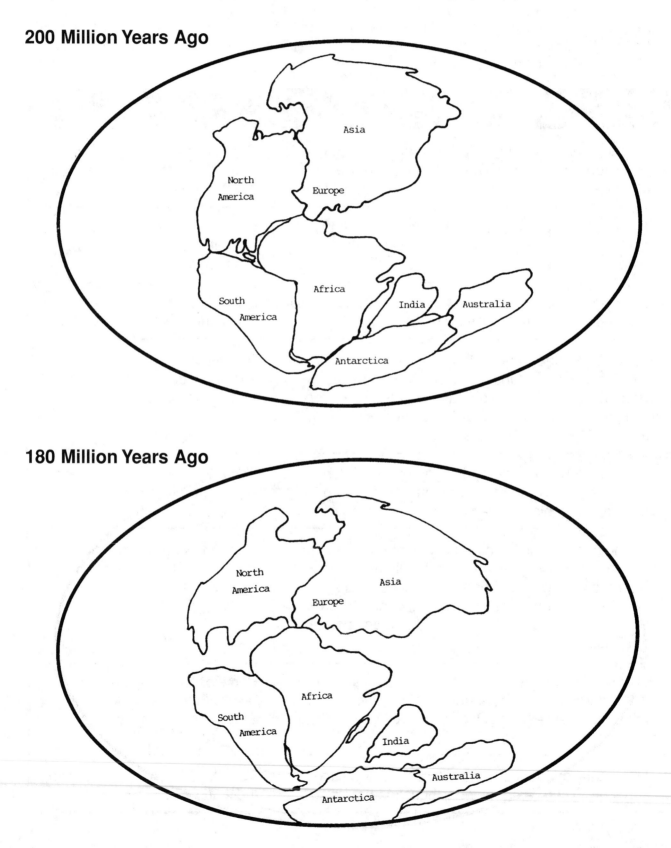

180 Million Years Ago

Cracked Earth (cont.)

Earth's Continents: Then, Now, and Beyond (cont.)

135 Million Years Ago

65 Million Years Ago

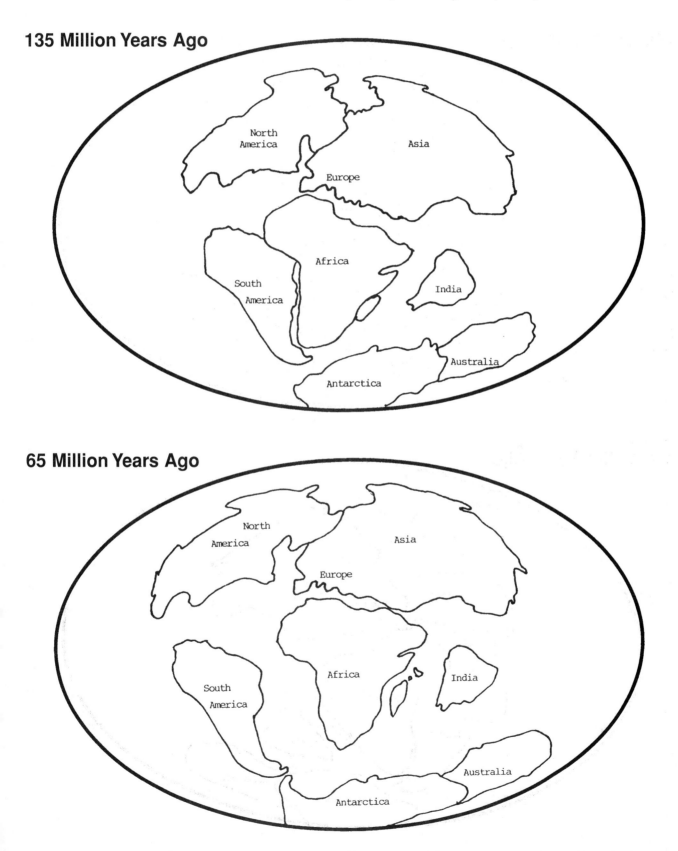

Cracked Earth *(cont.)*

Earth's Continents: Then, Now, and Beyond (cont.)

Today

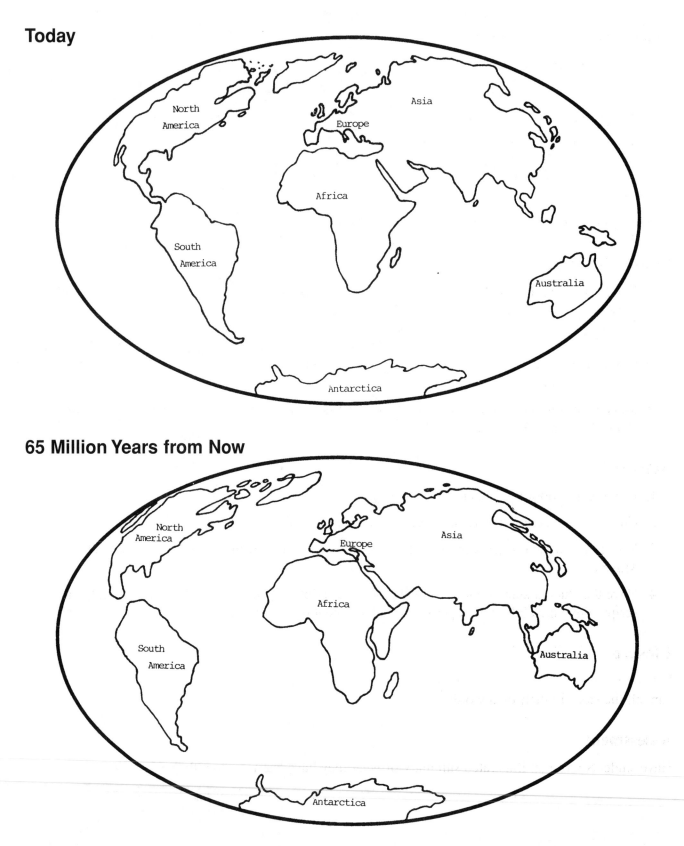

65 Million Years from Now

Walk Through the Rock Cycle

Overview: *Students use a model of the rock cycle to walk on as they discover how the three types of rocks are created and recycled.*

Materials

- large white bedsheet
- permanent ink felt pens
- transparency of The Rock Cycle (page 27)
- Rock Cycle Script (page 26)
- five pieces of 5" x 8" (13 cm x 20 cm) cardboard
- pencils
- crayons (gray, brown, green, red)

Lesson Preparation

- Pin the sheet to a wall and project the transparency on it so that it fills the bedsheet. Using pencil, trace the picture, including captions and numbers.
- Lay the sheet on a table and trace over the outlines and captions with black permanent pen.
- Color the igneous rock gray, the sedimentary rock brown, and the metamorphic rock green. The lava and magma should be red.
- Make signs on the cardboard to read as follows: *Igneous Rock*, *Sedimentary Rock*, *Metamorphic Rock*, *Lava*, and *Magma*.

Activity

1. Place on the floor the bedsheet with the rock cycle diagram on it.
2. Gather the students around the sides and bottom of the diagram.
3. Select one student to walk through the diagram. Give the student the card which is labeled *Magma*.
4. Have the student stand on #1 and read aloud the script. The child should move as directed in the script. Give the child the proper signs that are mentioned in the script.

Closure

Let additional students walk through the rock cycle. This can be done without the script so the students can tell the story in their own words.

Assessment

Have students write an illustrated summary of what they have learned about the rock cycle.

Walk Through the Rock Cycle *(cont.)*

Rock Cycle Script

1. You are *magma* under Earth's crust, below the floor of the ocean. Since your temperature is 1,600° F (870° C), you are semiliquid rock. You are under tremendous pressure from the hot magma below, as it rises from deep near the center of Earth. Now, you are being squeezed like toothpaste from a tube, and you flow out of a crack in the crust and onto the ocean floor.

2. As you break through the crust and meet the ocean water, you begin to cool. You are *lava* now, still hot enough to be semiliquid, so you ooze across the ocean floor getting thicker and thicker as you cool off.

3. You have cooled enough to become *igneous rock*, and you are added to the top and sides of the crustal plate under the ocean. Shells from dead animals fall to the floor of the ocean and pile up on top of you. More and more and more layers of shells and sand are piled up on you until they are squeezed together and turn into sedimentary rock. Since you are being pressed so hard by the sedimentary rock, you change from igneous rock to *metamorphic rock*.

4. The plate you are on is gradually moving, pushed along by more magma coming up through the crust just as you did. In many millions of years, you travel to the edge of the continent which is on another plate. Now the plate you are on begins to dive under the continental plate.

5. It is getting much hotter again, and you start to melt back into *magma*. You flow under the crust until you reach another large chamber.

6. You are inside a large chamber deep under a volcano. The pressure of the magma under you is pushing on you again, forcing you to rise up the throat of the volcano.

7. As you rise in the volcano, you begin to lose some of your heat and become thicker and turn into lava, but you are still not rock. Suddenly, the pressure is building behind you, and you are rising faster and faster!

8. You are pushed out of the top of the volcano and begin to flow down its steep side toward the ocean. Some of the material that came out with you has turned to fine ash and rises in a huge gray cloud over the volcano.

9. As you roll down the volcano's side, you run into the ocean. Oh! That feels better. Since you are still hot lava, you turn the water to boiling temperature, and it hisses and gives off steam. Your temperature changes very quickly, and you turn into pieces of rock. This is *igneous rock*, but you are in the form of sand because you cooled so quickly.

10. Millions of years later you are rolled to the ocean floor and begin to pile up with other sand and shells. As more layers are added, you are pressed into *sedimentary rock*. Your journey does not end here, however. You are on a plate going under the continental plate where you will be remelted and may have a trip to the center of Earth before rising through the crust again.

The Rock Cycle

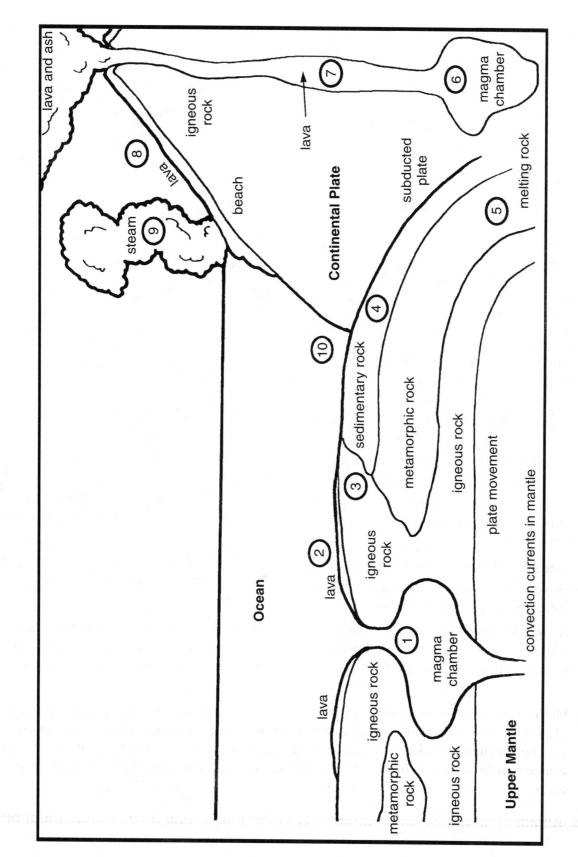

Shifting Crust

Overview: *Students will simulate the layers of rock in Earth's crust.*

Materials (per group)

- 3 pieces whole wheat bread
- smooth peanut butter
- plastic spreading knife
- transparency and copies of page 29
- transparency of page 27

- copies of page 30
- strawberry jam
- 2 Tbs. (30 g) melted plain chocolate bar
- waxed paper and napkin or paper towel

Lesson Preparation

Melt the chocolate bars in the microwave or over boiling water on a hot plate.

Activity

1. Review the transparency of page 27.

2. Have the students wash their hands and then divide them into small groups. Distribute the materials to each group.

3. Instruct the students to spread the waxed paper in the middle of their work areas and put the slices of bread on it. Have them work together to make a sandwich as follows:

   Spread a thin layer of chocolate on a slice of bread and spread peanut butter over it.

   Spread a thin layer of chocolate on a second slice of bread and spread jam over it.

4. Explain to the students what each material represents.

   Chocolate—igneous rock that was melted and forced between layers of rock.

   Peanut Butter—metamorphic rock, made by rock changed through pressure and heat.

   Jam—sedimentary rock with seeds being sedimentary rocks deposited in the ocean

   Bread—more sedimentary layers

Chocolate:
Igneous Rock

Jam:
Sedimentary Layer

Peanut Butter:
Metamorphic Rock

Chocolate: Igneous Rock

Bread: Sedimentary Layer

Closure

- Tell the students to put their bread together into a sandwich, with the bottom layer being the bread with peanut butter on it. Have them slice their sandwich in half. Show the transparency of The Movement of the Earth's Crust (page 29) and discuss it. Give a copy of it and the Sandwich Faults activity sheet (page 30), to each group and let them manipulate their sandwich to demonstrate the three types of faults. As they do so, have them draw each of these on the Sandwich Faults worksheet. Discuss the drawings with the students.

Shifting Crust *(cont.)*

The Movement of the Earth's Crust

The movement of the earth's crust is called *faulting*. This movement of the crust causes earthquakes. The three main types of faults are normal faulting, reverse faulting, and strike-slip faulting. All three are shown below.

Normal Fault: Two blocks of the earth's crust move apart from each other. One block may also drop below the other.

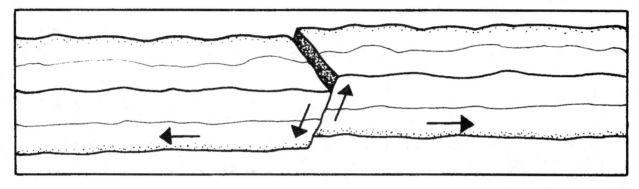

Reverse Fault: Two blocks push together, and one is pushed under the other. This is called *subduction*.

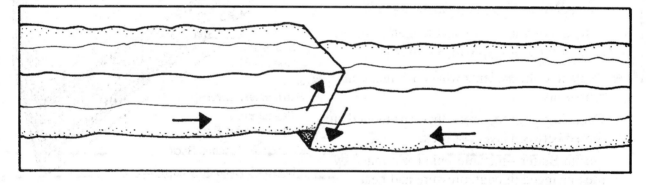

Strike-slip Fault: The two blocks slide past each other, but neither moves up or down.

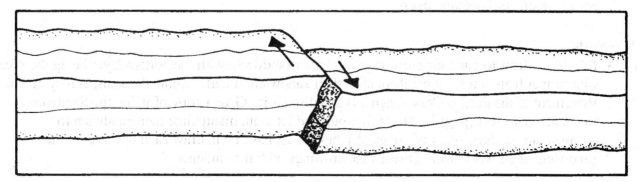

Shifting Crust *(cont.)*

Sandwich Faults

To the Students: Move your sandwich layer to show the type of faults explained in the pictures on page 29.

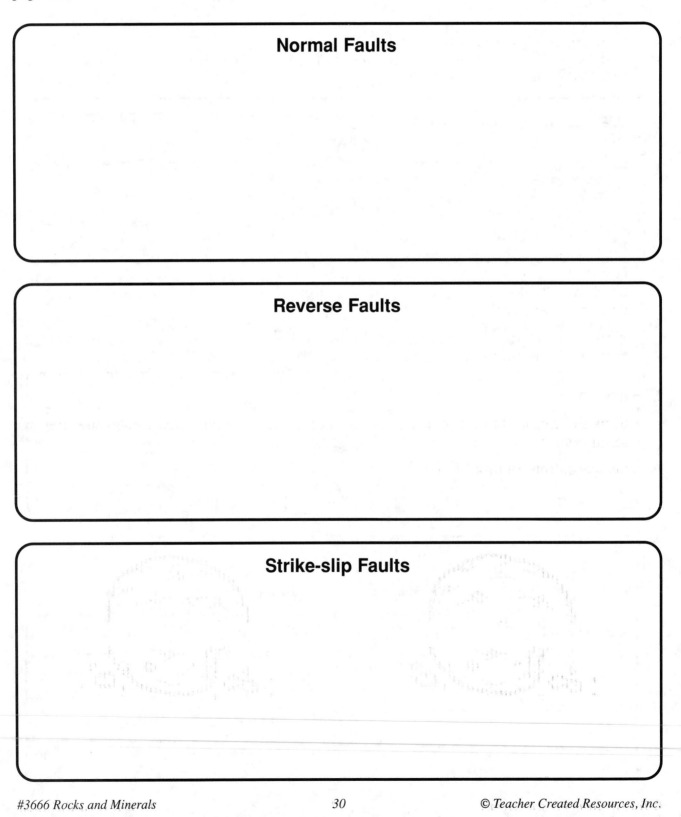

Normal Faults

Reverse Faults

Strike-slip Faults

Rock or Mineral?

Overview: *Students will discover the difference between rocks and minerals by using cookies.*

Materials

- cookies containing a variety of ingredients (e.g., colored M&M™ candies, raisins, chocolate chips, nuts)
- transparency and copies of What's in My Cookie? (page 32)
- mineral specimens
- rock specimens

Activity

1. Show students the examples of minerals and rocks. Tell them we often call all of these rocks but that the activity they are about to do will show them the difference.

2. Distribute a cookie and worksheet to each student. Explain that the cookie is like a rock, made up of many minerals.

3. Have students divide their cookies in half and put one half aside, to eat later. Let them begin to look in the cookie for ingredients which represent the minerals (e.g., raisins). Use the transparency to demonstrate how they pull the minerals out of the cookie and place them in different boxes on page 30.

4. After all the "minerals" have been placed on their worksheets, have the students tell you what they found. List the names on the board and have the students write these on page 32.

Closure

- Show the students the rock specimens and point out some of the different minerals which they can see in them.
- Let the students eat their "rocks."

Rock or Mineral? *(cont.)*

What's in My Cookie?

Pretend your cookie is a rock and pull it apart to find the "minerals" inside it. Put each different mineral in a box. After you have taken out all the "minerals," write what they are on the line in the boxes.

_____	_____	_____
_____	_____	_____

Homemade Rocks

Overview: *Students will make simulated rocks.*

Materials

- parent letter (page 34)
- play dough (Each child needs an amount about the size of a golf ball.)
- materials to mix into the play dough (See parent letter for suggestions.)
- 10 inches (25 cm) of string
- rock specimens which students bring from home

Lesson Preparation

Several days prior to doing this activity, send home the parent letter requesting materials to use to make the simulated rocks.

Activity

1. Distribute a lump of play dough to each student and have each knead the lump until it is soft.

2. Tell students to slowly mix the play dough with the things they brought to represent minerals.

3. Each student should add another thin layer of play dough to the rocks. This represents weathering in nature, often hiding the minerals inside the rocks.

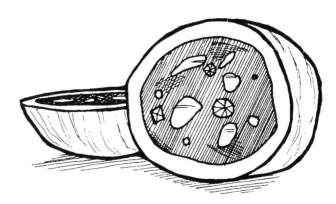

Closure

- Give each student a piece of string. Have each student tie each end to a separate pencil so that about four inches (10 cm) of string is left between the pencils. Show them how to use this device to cut their rocks in half.

- Let students examine the cross section of their rocks and look at the minerals which they can now see that were not visible on the surface before. Have them compare their simulated rocks to the classroom rock collection.

Parent Letter for Simulated Rock Materials

Date_____

Dear Parents,

Our class has studied the difference between *rocks* and *minerals*. The students learned that a rock is made up of two or more minerals, while a mineral is all the same material. We used cookies to represent rocks and pulled them apart to find all the "minerals" in them.

Our next activity is to make simulated rocks from play dough and things students bring from home. These items should be small since the lump of play dough will be about the size of a golf ball. Items which would be good to use are as follows:

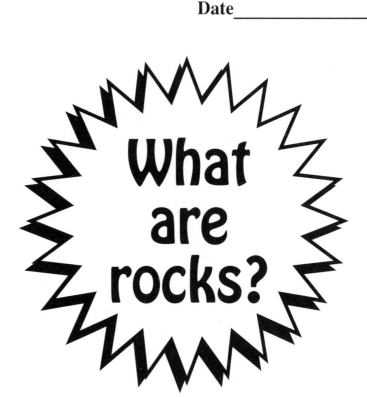

- small chips of rocks, such as aquarium rocks

- synthetic jewels from old jewelry

- marbles

- small pebbles

- charcoal pieces

- scraps of aluminum foil

The students also need a variety of actual rock specimens to compare with their simulated rocks. If you have any interesting rocks you are willing to lend our class, we would appreciate having them for our display table. Of course, these will be returned to you as soon as our study ends.

When the students are finished making their rocks, they will cut them open and compare them with the actual rock specimens. They will keep their simulated rocks at the end of our study.

Thank you for your help in making this an exciting activity for your child.

Cordially,

_____

Minerals

Teacher Information

Rocks are made up of two or more minerals. Minerals are created from elements on Earth and are found in soil and rocks. Many of these same minerals make up the crust of the rocky planets of Mercury, Venus, Mars, and moons of the planets in our solar system.

Mineralogists define minerals as substances which . . .

- formed naturally.
- are made of materials that were never alive.
- have the same chemical makeup wherever they are found.
- have atoms which are arranged in regular patterns and form solid units called crystals.

By this definition, substances such as coal, petroleum and natural gas, or pearls and coral are not minerals since they were formed by once living plants and animals. Substances such as calcium, iron, and phosphorus, which are found in food and water, are often called minerals, but mineralogists do not consider them minerals.

Minerals are usually a compound of two or more elements. Some minerals, such as gold and sulfur, however, are made of only one element. The most common elements which form minerals are oxygen and silicon. Others include aluminum, iron, sodium, potassium, and magnesium. There are about 2,000 known minerals. Common minerals can be recognized by some characteristics such as the following:

Color: Minerals are found in a variety of colors due to the chemicals in them. For instance, quartz occurs in many hues but may also be colorless. Some minerals are always the same color—e.g., galena is metallic gray, sulfur is yellow, azurite is blue, and malachite is green. A fresh surface is needed to see the true color since weathering may hide it.

Luster: The amount of light reflected from a mineral's surface is its luster. Luster may be described as glassy, metallic, shiny, dull, waxy, satiny, or greasy.

Streak Color: Some minerals leave a colored streak when rubbed across a piece of unglazed white tile. The streak color may not be the same as the mineral's color. For example, hematite may be black to brown, but its streak is red-brown.

Texture: Texture is the "feel" of the mineral's surface when it is rubbed. This may be rough, smooth, bumpy, or soapy.

Hardness: Although all minerals are hard, the surface varies in resistance to scratching. The Mohs hardness scale of 1 to 10 is applied to minerals. The hardness test is done with common materials which vary in hardness, such as a fingernail, penny, steel knife or nail, and glass. The hardness number is assigned depending upon which item will scratch the mineral's surface.

The activities in this section will develop the students' skills in identifying minerals through careful observation and by gathering data about the characteristics described above.

Minerals (cont.)

Sorting Minerals

Overview: *Using their shoes, students will learn how to sort by one characteristic.*

Materials

- one shoe from each student and one from the teacher
- decks of cards

Activity

1. Tell students you are going to sort them into groups and that you want them to see if they can guess how you are sorting them. Divide the students into groups by sex without letting the students know your system. Do this by calling one student at a time to a specific area in the room so they will join the boys' or girls' group.

2. After you have selected five students, ask the students if they have guessed the characteristic you are using to sort the students. Ask the students if they know of any other way to sort people.

3. Tell the students that they are going to learn how to sort their shoes. Seat the class in a large circle on the floor and have each remove one shoe. Place these in the center of the circle, along with a shoe from the teacher, so that all can see the shoes. Have the students talk to their neighbors to discuss ways in which the shoes could be sorted (*color*, *size*, *material*, etc.).

4. Ask the students to tell some of the ways they thought of for sorting the shoes and list these on the board. Choose one of the characteristics suggested by the students and have volunteers sort the shoes by this method.

5. Select another characteristic but show the students that it would make the job of sorting very difficult if they used both the new and old characteristics to sort the shoes. Place the shoes in the center again and have other volunteers sort the shoes again by the new characteristics.

Closure

- Divide the students into groups of three or four and give each group a deck of cards from which the jokers have been removed. Tell the students to sort their cards by one characteristic chosen by the group. Have them share the different ways each group discovered for sorting the cards and list these on the board.

- Continue to have them use the cards to find more ways of sorting them.

Minerals (cont.)

Identifying Minerals

Overview: *Students will begin to develop methods for identifying minerals.*

Materials

- parent letter (page 38)
- rock and mineral specimens
- pictures of minerals
- sets of eight mineral specimens: *calcite, galena, graphite, hematite, magnetite, obsidian, quartz,* and *talc* (Mineral specimens are available from the Delta Education ESS catalog. See Resources section.)

Lesson Preparation

- Send home the parent letter to invite them to bring or send mineral specimens to school so they may be displayed in the classroom. As the specimens arrive, arrange them on a display table. Do not add identification labels at this time.
- Make up sets of the minerals listed above for small groups of students to use.

Activity

1. Review the activity of shoe sorting with the students. Tell them that in this activity they will be sorting mineral specimens.

2. Divide the students into groups of three or four. Distribute a set of minerals to each group. Tell them to look at and handle the minerals and decide how they can be sorted, using only characteristics chosen by the group. Explain that they should place the minerals in different areas on their table, according to the characteristics. Let them know that when they have finished they will be moving to another group's area to see how they sorted their minerals. Tell them that if the other group can tell how their minerals were sorted, they did a good job.

3. Let the students sort their minerals. Monitor them to be sure they are using only one characteristic and that they are setting each group of minerals apart to show how they were sorted.

Closure

- Have the students go to another group and determine what characteristics they used to sort the minerals. Write these on the board.
- Let each group re-sort the minerals done by the other group, using a different characteristic. List the new methods for sorting on the board.

To the Teacher: Do not let students sort by a characteristic which would vary, such as size of the pieces of minerals. They should discover that the minerals can be sorted by *color, texture, luster,* and possibly *density*.

Minerals *(cont.)*

Parent Letter for Mineral Specimens

Date_____

Dear Parents,

During our study of rocks and minerals, we have examined sand and soil to learn where they come from. We have also learned about *igneous*, *metamorphic*, and *sedimentary* rocks and discovered how these rocks are constantly being changed and recycled.

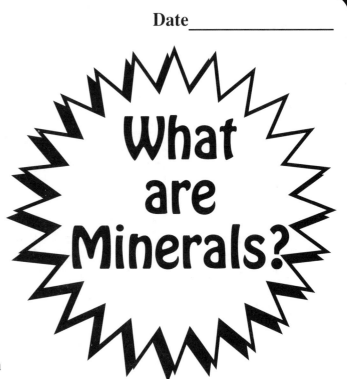

Now, we are going to study the minerals which make up the rocks. It would be very interesting for the children to see a wide variety of minerals. If you have any which we could display in our classroom, we would appreciate borrowing them for a short time. Please bring them to school or send them with your child. If possible, please label the minerals so the students can see their names. The minerals will be placed on a display table where students are permitted to look but not touch them, so we will take good care of the specimens.

Following is a partial list of minerals, some of which you might have to help us in our study:

• pyrite	• chert	• mica
• gypsum	• garnet	• petrified wood
• agate	• halite	• malachite
• amethyst	• jade	• turquoise

Your mineral specimens will be returned to you by_____ when our study ends. You are welcome to come visit our classroom and see our display of minerals, as well as watch us in action while we do activities to learn about minerals.

Be sure to ask your child what he or she is doing in science class while learning about rocks and minerals.

Cordially,

_____

Minerals *(cont.)*

Matching Minerals

Overview: *Students will describe mineral specimens.*

Materials

- sets of eight mineral specimens
- transparency and copies of page 40

Activity

1. Review the list of mineral characteristics students discovered in the previous lesson.

2. Divide the students into groups of three or four students and distribute a set of minerals and copies of page 40 to each group.

3. Show the transparency of the worksheet. Explain the terms *luster* and *texture* and write examples of these on the board. (See the teacher information on page 35.) Write examples of colors students see in the eight minerals on the board.

4. Select one of the mineral specimens and show it to the students. Place it on page 40 in the #1 position. Have the students help you write a description of its color, luster, and texture.

5. Explain that each member of the group will pick one of the minerals and write a description of its color, luster, and texture on the work sheet. Tell the students that they may not choose the mineral that was used for the demonstration. Be sure they know that they are only to describe one mineral per group member, rather than describing all eight minerals.

6. Let them know that when all have finished their work they will go to another group's table, just as in the last class, to see if they can match their minerals with their descriptions. The group will be considered successful if the other group can match all of their minerals.

7. Monitor the students as they work, assisting when needed. Be sure the students are as specific as possible with their descriptions.

Closure

- When all students have finished describing their minerals, have them put the minerals in a pile next to page 40 and move to another group's table. They should read the descriptions and match the minerals.

- Have each group return to their own table and check on the matching to see if it was done correctly. To help students see how they can improve on their descriptions, discuss any of the minerals which were not matched.

Minerals (cont.)

Student Data Sheet

Names of Group Members: _____

Each member of the group should pick a different mineral to describe. Next to one of the numbers, write the color, luster, and texture of that mineral.

Mineral	Color	Luster	Texture
1			
2			
3			
4			

Minerals *(cont.)*

Naming Minerals

Overview: *Students will identify the eight mineral specimens.*

Materials

- sets of eight minerals
- transparency and copies of page 42
- streak plates (Streak plates are unglazed tiles. These may be purchased through ESS Catalog.)

Activity

1. Review what the students learned in the Matching Minerals lesson (pages 39–40). Tell them that they are going to find out the names of the eight minerals they have been using.

2. Divide the students into their small groups and distribute a set of minerals and the identification key to each group.

3. Show them the transparency of the identification key and select one of the descriptions to use as a demonstration of how to use the key. Let the students find the mineral which matches the description you have selected and tell them to place that mineral on its name. Check to see if all have been able to find the mineral.

4. Tell the students to divide the remaining minerals among their group members. They should use the descriptions to find the names for their minerals and place them on the chart.

5. Monitor the students as they work to be sure they are matching the minerals correctly. If they have incorrectly matched any of the minerals, remove them from the key and have them try again.

Closure

- Have students identify some of the display minerals (if available) which are the same as the eight minerals they have been using.

- Add the labels to the display minerals so the students can now see the mineral names.

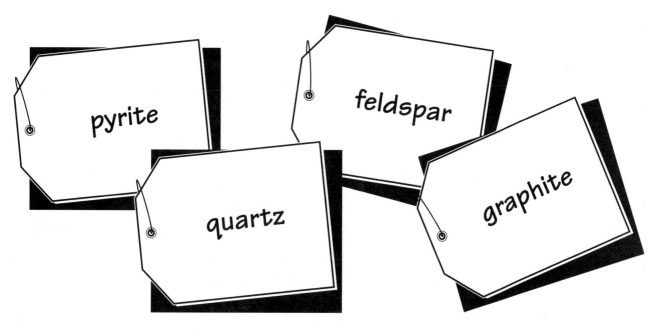

Minerals (cont.)

Student's Mineral Identification Key

Match your minerals to these descriptions and then find their names.

Mineral	Color	Luster	Texture	Streak	Hardness
calcite	tan and white	shiny and glassy	smooth	white or pink	penny 3
galena	silver	metallic and shiny	smooth to rough	dark gray or black	penny 3
graphite	dark gray	dull	smooth to bumpy	black or dark gray	fingernail 1
quartz	milky white	shiny and glassy	smooth to bumpy	white	none more than 6.5
obsidian	black	glassy	smooth with sharp edges	none	none more than 6.5
hematite	reddish brown	dull	rough	red brown	fingernail to nail 1-6
magnetite	gray or black	dull	rough	black or dark gray	none above 7
talc	light gray, may have some white	dull	smooth, feels like soap	white	fingernail 1

Crystal Creations

Observing Crystals

Teacher Information

Most minerals are formed in a liquid state and develop crystal structures as they solidify. That means they have solid, regular shapes. These shapes vary from simple to complex, from very tiny to extremely large. Some minerals (gems) form beautiful crystals which we use as jewelry. The most famous gems are diamonds, rubies, and emeralds. Crystals may vary in color, depending upon chemical content. For example, diamonds may be blue, white, or pink, as well as other shades.

Overview: *Students will observe crystal forms of salt, alum, Epsom salt, and cupric sulfate.*

Materials

- eight disposable five-ounce (160 mL) cups
- eight disposable spoons
- very hot water
- food coloring
- magnifying lenses (one per student)
- transparent or double-sided tape

- 3" x 5" (8 cm x 13 cm) file cards
- eight petri dishes or small saucers
- crystal forms of salt, alum, Epsom salt, and cupric sulfate
- clear tape

Note: Petri dishes are available from Delta Education. Epsom salt and alum are available in drug stores. Cupric sulfate is poisonous and should therefore be handled with care. It can be obtained from Flint Scientific or a high school chemistry teacher. (See page 48 for information on science suppliers.)

Lesson Preparation

Make sets of four cards, each with a different crystal specimen adhered with double-sided tape. Since cupric sulfate is poisonous, adhere it to the cards by placing the clear tape over the crystals. Label each card with the name of its crystal (e.g., alum, Epsom salt). Each group of students will need a set of cards.

Activity

1. Divide students into small groups and distribute a set of file cards and four magnifiers to each group.
2. Have students look closely at the crystal shapes. Have them draw the shape of each crystal on a piece of paper.
3. Explain that these crystals form naturally and that you are going to show them how they become crystals.
   - Pour about three teaspoons (15 mL) of hot water into a cup.
   - Add about ¼ teaspoon (1 g) of cupric sulfate to the water.
   - Stir with the spoon until it dissolves completely. If necessary, continue to add more cupric sulfate until no more will dissolve.
   - Pour all of this solution into the petri dish or small saucer.
   - Set the dish on a tray with a label nearby of the chemical used.
   - Repeat with other chemicals, using a new cup and spoon each time.
4. Tell the students that they will be watching these dishes during the next few days to see what appears.

Crystal Creations (cont.)

Observing Crystals (cont.)

Closure

- After the water evaporates, the crystals of salt, etc., should appear in the bottoms of the dishes. The slower the evaporation rate, the larger the crystals will be. When they have formed, have students examine them with magnifiers and compare them with what they saw earlier. They should see that the same shapes appear as they did before the solids were dissolved.

- Explain that this is just what happens in nature. If available, show examples of natural crystals such as quartz or calcite.

- Tell students that crystals may be of different colors, depending upon what chemicals may mix with them as they form. If available, show the students natural crystals which may be the same shape but different color, such as clear, milky white, or black quartz. Tell them this can be simulated by using food coloring as the chemical added to their homemade crystals. Mix up a solution of salt and add a few drops of food coloring. Pour this into a dish to evaporate. When the salt crystals form, they will be the color which was added to them but have the cubic shape of salt. Make colored solutions of Epsom salts and alum, using different colors to show that they also can be various colors.

Crystal Shapes

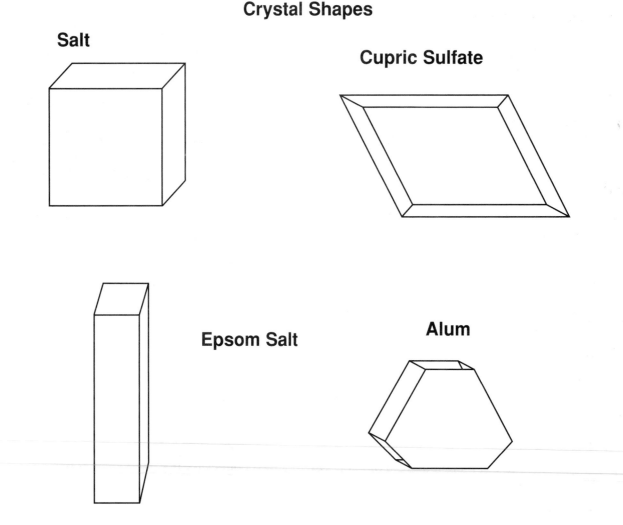

Salt

Cupric Sulfate

Epsom Salt

Alum

Crystal Creations *(cont.)*

Simulated Geodes

Teacher Information

A very special kind of crystal formation takes place inside some rocks. When such rocks are broken open, beautiful crystals may cover the cavity within the rock. Water with dissolved mineral in it filled the hollow rock at one time. When the water evaporated, it left behind the crystals of the mineral. These rocks are usually roughly spherical and may be 2 to 6 inches (5 to 15 cm) in diameter. They are called geodes. Crystals of quartz are often found inside geodes. Finding a geode is like discovering a treasure chest.

Overview: *Students will make simulated geodes from nut shells.*

Materials

- walnut shell halves
- large paper cup of hot water
- salt, alum, or Epsom salt
- red, green, or blue food coloring
- spoons
- magnifying lenses
- examples of geodes

Activity

1. Divide the students into groups. Distribute a cup of hot water and salt, alum, or Epsom salt to each group. Supply them with a spoon and a container of food coloring.

2. Have them pour salt, alum, or Epsom salt into the hot water, adding the solid until no more will dissolve.

3. They should add a few drops of food coloring and then pour the solution into the walnut shell. The shell should not overflow with the liquid.

4. Have the groups set these aside and allow the liquid to evaporate for the next few days so the crystals will form.

Closure

- Have the students compare the geodes they have "grown" with examples of actual geodes.

- Explain the teacher information to the students so they can see that natural geodes form much like the ones they have just made.

Crystal Creations *(cont.)*

Crystal Garden

Overview: *Students will observe a chemical crystal garden grow.*

Materials

- small container such as margarine tub
- piece of sponge or charcoal, about the size of a golf ball
- dropper bottles of red, green, blue, and yellow food coloring
- household ammonia
- water
- salt
- laundry bluing (found in laundry section of grocery or drug stores)
- glass jar for mixing
- measuring cup and spoons
- large spoon for stirring mixture

Demonstration

1. This demonstration needs to be done outside or in a well-ventilated classroom to avoid breathing ammonia fumes. Mix the following in a jar to make the chemical solution:
   - six tablespoons (90 mL) each of hot water and laundry bluing
   - three tablespoons (45 mL) salt
   - one tablespoon (15 mL) ammonia
2. Place the sponge or charcoal in the center of the margarine tub.
3. Mix the salt and hot water until it dissolves.
4. Add bluing and ammonia and stir into the mixture.
5. Pour this solution over the sponge or charcoal, completely covering it.
6. Place a few drops of food coloring on the surface of the sponge or charcoal. Add different colored drops in various areas, leaving some without any coloring.
7. Place the bowl in a location where it will not be disturbed but can be observed by students. Crystals will begin to form in 1 to 12 hours, depending on the amount of humidity in the atmosphere and the temperature. The slower the liquid evaporates, the larger the crystals will become. The odor of the ammonia and bluing will persist until the liquid evaporates.
8. Do not touch the crystal garden once crystals begin to form. The crystals are very fragile.

Closure

Have students compare the crystals grown in this garden with the salt, alum, Epsom salt, and cupric sulfate crystals grown in the Crystal Creations and Simulated Geodes lessons. They will see that these crystals look more like snow and are very soft.

Extenders

- Grow the chemical crystals on different surfaces, such as rock, leaf, cloth.
- Try making the solution without the salt, ammonia, or water and see if crystals will form.

Making a Rock-and-Mineral Journal

Overview: *Students will create a cover for their rocks-and-minerals journal.*

Materials

- light-colored file folders or heavy construction paper
- colored pens or crayons
- all data sheets completed by the students in this study
- copies of pages 18, 26, and 27 for each student

Activity

1. Distribute a folder or folded construction paper to each student. Distribute the worksheets the students have completed during this study. Give them copies of the diagrams of the earth's layers and rock cycle (pages 26 and 27).

2. Discuss some of the things students have learned during their study of rocks and minerals.

3. Tell the students to draw pictures on the fronts and backs of their covers to show some of the things they learned.

4. Monitor the students as they work to help inspire them as needed.

5. Have each student write a brief story, pretending to be a rock going through changes to become igneous, metamorphic, and sedimentary rock. Tell them to make pictures to help them tell their stories.

Closure

Display the journals in the classroom and let students share them with their parents and other students.

Teacher and Student Resources

Related Books

Cole, Joanna. *The Magic School Bus ® Inside the Earth.* Scholastic Inc., 1989. Ms. Frizzle takes her students on another zany adventure, this time into the center of the Earth.

Davidson, Keay and A. R. Williams. "Under the Skin: Hot Theories on the Center of the Earth." *National Geographic,* January 1996, Vol. 189, No. 1. Outstanding drawings depict information regarding current theories of the interior of the earth, including motion within the mantle. Back issues may be ordered online from **http://www.nationalgeographic.com/**

Young, Ruth M. *Science Literature Unit: The Magic School Bus ® Inside the Earth.* Teacher Created Materials, Inc., 1995. **http://www.teachercreated.com/**

This book is filled with hands-on activities which bring to life the adventures of Ms. Frizzle's students in Joanna Cole's book of the same title.

Suppliers of Science Materials

Delta Education (800) 282-9560 Request a catalog of materials or order online at their Web site. **http://www.delta-education.com/corp/info/ordernow.html**

Supplies a wide variety of materials to support hands-on science in all areas from elementary to middle school, including mineral specimens. Request the Elementary Science Study (ESS) catalog for the mineral specimens.

Great Explorations in Math and Science (GEMS)
http://www.lhs.berkeley.edu/GEMS/gemsguides.html

Directly from the Lawrence Hall of Science at UC Berkeley comes great teacher guides in a wide range of science topics. Check out their Web site to see all that is available.

National Science Resources Center **http://www.si.edu/nsrc/**

Resources for Teaching Elementary Science. National Science Resources Center, National Academy Press, Washington, D.C., 1996. This outstanding resource guide to hands-on inquiry-centered elementary science curriculum materials and resources. Each reference in this guide has been carefully evaluated and is fully described, including addresses.

Read this book online or order it from: **http://www.nap.edu/catalog/4966.html**

National Science Teachers Association(NSTA) (800) 277-5300

http://www.nsta.org/ or the online catalog of materials at **http://store.nsta.org/**

Provides books, posters, and software related to astronomy and other sciences.

A monthly professional journal, the bimonthly NSTA Reports, discounts at the regional and national conventions and annual catalog of materials are offered.